DOVE
ON
FIRE

DOVE ON FIRE

Poems on Peace, Justice and Ecology

CECIL RAJENDRA

Illustrations by Jose Venturelli

THE RISK BOOK SERIES

WCC Publications, Geneva

Most of the poems in this volume have been selected from the following anthologies of Cecil Rajendra's poems:

Bones & Feathers, Heinemann Educational Books (Asia) Ltd, 1978.

Refugees and Other Despairs, Choice Books Pte Ltd, 1980.

Hour of Assassins and Other Poems, Bogle-L'ouverture Publications Ltd, 1983.

Child of the Sun, Bogle-L'ouverture Publications Ltd, 1986.

We are grateful to the publishers for giving us permission to reproduce them in this volume.

Cover design: Michael Dominguez

ISBN 2-8254-0899-9

© 1987 WCC Publications, World Council of Churches, 150 route de Ferney, 1211 Geneva 20, Switzerland

No. 33 in the Risk book series

Printed in Switzerland

For my children

SHAKILA and YASUNARI

Contents

Preface

We live in a world of contradictions, both threatening and terrifying. We preach conservation, yet each year lay waste millions of acres of forest; we advocate peace, yet arm ourselves to the teeth...

Like others, I can make little sense of this world which I both love and loathe. Yet some attempt must be made to come to grips with these nightmare realities. Not to do so would be a supreme act of cowardice, an abnegation of our duties as responsible human beings.

So we live and we fight and try to keep a toehold on our sanity. At the heart of the matter is survival — both personal and universal.

These poems mushroomed in the froth and ferment of one man's struggle for survival.

I did not write these poems; they wrote themselves!

CECIL RAJENDRA

New Year's Day

Today
the resolutions
(and so little time
        for so many intentions)

I will be good
I will work hard
I will beat
my wife less often
I shall snarl less
Smile more
I will be a little more
generous with my affections

I will diet
I'll do my exercises
I will cut my drinking
Give up smoking
I will be a little less
boring in my conversations

I will stop the bombing
Start negotiating
Halt the killing
Commence healing
I will try
not to hurt man or animal

I will... I will...

Today's
that day
for resolutions
and the resolutions
come flooding in
for tomorrow
Tomorrow
the betrayals begin

Defence

Who will quarrel with our right
to protect family and country?
Who will quarrel with the right
of self-preservation? To defend
ourselves is innate reflex action.

And defence was that: vigilance,
a guard dog, a moat and a padlock
ducking or warding off a blow
keeping a stick and stone handy.

But look how we've evolved: an open
eye has become an undercover spy,
bugs, stratagems and red-alert systems.
Stones and sticks have ballooned
into an armoury of grenades, rifles
bombs, bazookas and ballistic missiles.

Defence, no longer for self-preservation,
is now attack and invasion. Offence
has been decreed the best form of defence.
And defence is a trigger-happy army
led across borders by a mad general
fuelled by a stock of unlimited artillery.

Defence is flattening the homes
of your neighbours, for neighbours can
turn aggressors; slitting the wombs
of foreign women for they are poten-
tial breeders of alien children. Defence
is fire-bombing kindergartens for
toddlers may grow into enemy soldiers.

Defence is the midwife of Strontium-
90 and a nuclear factory; a monsoon
of agent orange, napalm, CX
and anthrax. Defence is a one-act
masque played on an empty
stage with gas-masks; or is it
a grand comic opera where a 10,000-
megaton aria rings the final curtain?

Yes, Defence is Death and Death and Death
for only death's the ultimate deterrent.

Concerns

Not that i am
not concerned;
i bleed as much
as the next man.

But the bomb's such
a remote happenstance
and there are other
pressing commitments:

there are those premiums
on our life insurance;
car, hire-purchase
and mortgage instalments.

Nest-eggs for the baby's
future Higher Education.
Ang-pows and New Year
clothes for the children.

Staff salaries, the cook,
maid and gardener's wages;
Annual fees and subs
to our Gourmet Club.

So many other concerns and
the bomb — like people prone
to spontaneous combustion —
is such a distant proposition.

Excuse me,
        i think our chicken's
                burning in the oven!

Home

"170 million abandoned children roam the cities of the third world. They have few options — vagrancy, crime, violence, despair and death. They are skinny, dirty, sick, ill-fed and weak."

Home is
rice and saltfish
and green mango pickles

a bowl of hot soup
after being caught in a drizzle

Home is
laughter and toys
and comforting arms of mother

tears being brushed away
playground bruises kissed better

Home is
socks, shoes, schoolbags
and crispy shirts in naphthalene

flannel blankets and fluffy
pillows and warm pink dreams

Home is
a fortress against
fear, thunder and the bogeyman

a sanctuary from terror
night sirens and the policeman.

Home
is the place
this continent
of damned children
will never taste!

The morning after

Acupunctured by silver
skewers of rain
the earth revivifies...

The morning after
last night's shower
unlocked from earth
a family of amanita
mushrooms assemble
under our hibiscus.

The children explode
with delight
                    clap
their hands and talk
of princesses and frogs
and other wondrous things.

And my mind hurtles
to another scenario
equally fantastical...

that morning after
the Generals' bacchanal
of giant mushrooms
when the sky drunk
with roaring fireballs
retches her black rain

that morning after
and all mornings after...
acupunctured by needles
of silent radiation

how many children
will there be to dance
clap hands with glee
how many
of our children will there be?

Cows, clams and cynics

You give a sack of rice
here, a handful of coins
there, a pile of blankets...
Then, somewhere else the tanks
thunder through fences.
Another people splinter
like inferior matches and again
the needless pain spills over.

Against the behemoth jugger-
naut of History, the precision
of computers, we have no answer.
All we have is a small voice,
an imprecise heart, and it
takes so much less than an
atom blast to muffle the human voice, detonate that heart.

Beseiged, then, by textbooks
of History, routed by roulette
odds, harpooned on all fronts
by nudging, smirking cynics,
wouldn't the shaman say
the only rational alter-
native is a bovine indifference,
retreat into an oyster silence?

So, take your poems and burn them!
Take your banner and stuff it!
Take your screams and cork them!
Take your conscience and snuff it!
If the world blows, let it go;
Let us all turn pragmatic.
Why save the world anyway —
A world of the cow, clam and cynic.

Immigrant
(for Rebecca and Rhina)

From mangrove and swamp her
        forefathers
hacked this rugged land;
        laid tracks
townships, roads and ports.
        With wife
and child in tow, sweated
        blood
in tin mine and rubber estate
        to give
this country its spine of steel.

In the teeth of disease, death
        torture
her fathers fought from the
        heart
of our deepest, darkest jungle
        to wrest
this land from the martial
        fist
of the occupying imperialist.

Her mothers' wit, inventiveness
        genius
enriched our language, culture
        cuisine
with cake, curry, kebaya, boria
        porcelain.

Her roots now so entwined with
                    strands
of this country's history/future
                    she felt
not one iota less than a full
                    citizen.
Till that fateful morning when
                    she awoke
to find herself branded **immigrant**.

More equal than others

There is the Constitution
and there is Parliament
and it is rumoured
that every citizen
is equal before the Law.

Then consider this:
for pinching a portion
of cheese from a market
a stripling is summarily
despatched to prison.

For the commission
of no crime save being
in possession of a gun
our hangman has swung
an indeterminate number
of our citizens to Nirvana.

Meanwhile, fattened bankers
play catch-us-if-you-can
after emptying the country's
coffers of over two billion;
and a Rt Hon. Minister
is accorded a royal pardon
for a cold premeditated murder.

There is the Constitution
and there is Parliament
and it is rumoured
that every citizen
is equal before the Law.

Political hues

The Emperor
always maintained
his administration
was unblemished *white*

The newspapers thought
it somewhat *grey*
said so in *black and white*

The Emperor saw *red*
turned *purple*, declared
the news *yellow*
shut the papers down
branded the now *blue*
editor a *pink* hack
and stuffed him into pyjamas —
regulation striped *white and black*!

Requiem for justice

A few candles are lit
on that altar
called "natural justice"
but the God is "procedure".

Homes/jobs do not matter,
if their papers were not
filed on time, or in order
they have no rights...

Beyond thumbprint/signature
our Lords on high chairs
cannot or will not see
lives twisted in agony.

An old woman's hut
jobs of factory workers —
all are nothing but
routine matters in Chambers:

Where, knowing the number
of your "enclosure"
often carries more weight
than any plea
                    for equity!

Proper attire

Saying it is cheaper
to plead guilty
than engage a lawyer,
unrepresented
the poor are herded
from lock-up
to dock to prison.
Guilt/innocence
no longer the question
just Dollars and Cents.

Meanwhile, members of our
honourable profession
(issued with a directive
on proper attire)
in white shirts and black ties
file into Court
with their well-heeled clients.

Have they come
to mourn the death of Justice?

This world

Moscow: A 17-year old Moscow girl has been arrested and interned in a psychiatric hospital for having joined demonstrations marking Human Rights Day.

Hongkong: A man who got carried away with the holiday spirit and gave away thousands of dollars will usher in the new year in a mental hospital.

A.F.P.

Where prisoners of conscience
waste forgotten in prisons
where the norm is torture
in extracting "confessions"...

To be generous
            is madness
To be humane
            insane.

Where nothing is ever given
without hope of a dividend;
and only money in the pocket
buys respect on the market...

To be generous
            is madness
To be humane
            insane

Where dogs of destruction
are decorated with medals;
and tightwad entrepreneurs
elevated to Finance Ministers...

To be generous
                    is madness
To be humane
                    insane

Professional hazards

I knot my tie
go to work
the paper-shifting
inanities begin.

Beyond this window
newspapers report
conflagrations
of blood and violence

In some city, where?
in some country there
they say the streets
are littered with corpses.

Here an old pen leaks
in crimson empathy
to smudge some
pettifogging affidavit.

Automaton-like i reach
for the correction fluid.
Would that universal blain
be expunged as neatly.

News at ten t.v. images
lines from the morning's paper
twist and twist in the brain
like a hoodlum's bearing-scraper.

Azania

As the overseas page
of yesterday's newspaper —
twisted into a thong
to start our garden bonfire —
splutters into flames...
the half-charred words
South Africa/Mandela
uncoil to sear my eye.

There is no escape...
your metamorphosis
through blood and fire
is mine too, AZANIA!
Our destinies are intertwined.

Waiting

Inside, time moves
    on chelonian feet
He weighs the hours
    chews the minutes
While on the outside
    the "gentlemen" who
put him there exclaim
    "tempus fugit!!"

Weeks, months, pass
    for them as fast
as a humming-bird's wingbeat
    as they hop from
this assembly to that
    rabbitting on and on
about the stability
    the equity of their system

He lies in gaol
    weighing the hours
chewing the minutes
    reviews the men
who put him there
    and smiles...
remembering an old tale
    about a tortoise and a hare

The humane voice

(for Hector Orlando Gomez, a press officer for a human rights group in Guatemala City, whose body was found one Sunday morning with his tongue removed.)

The cat
that got your tongue
had claws of steel.

In a jungle —
of glass or green —
the animal
with most muscle
is still king.

You spoke out
too long/too loud
Hector Orlando
on all those old-
fashioned freedoms
now no longer
in vogue in our
cities of expediency.

Thinking they
could silence you
they ripped
out your tongue;
but your voice
Hector Orlando
still sings
in this your hymn.

Menda city

In Menda city
there is no unemployment
nor any housing problem:
people live in fabrications
and work full-time as eye-
washers and window-dressers.

And there is no shortage
of food; kitchens everywhere
offer an expresso lip-service
of tossed flim-flams
and a glass of bunkum juice
with a side-order of humbugs.

But there is law and order
which is maintained by
weekly public hangings of
Articles of the Constitution.

And there's entertainment
in myriad discotheques
where young people
high on moonshine
do the clap-trap
and the shift and shuffle.

On the stock exchange
the candour deficit
is more than off-set
by the trade surplus
brought in by the export
of choice high grade lies.

The pews of Parliament
are filled with Mickey
Mouse cardboard cut-outs
(with speech bubbles)
saying: "AYE!" in unison;
while politicians queue
before all-night clinics
for their daily prescription
of bottled dissimulation
and canard prophylactics.

Truth is a refugee
from newspaper columns
in Menda city.
Honesty has been shunted
to neighbouring
slums and shanty towns
in Menda city —
where the sycophant is king!

The fan

(for Dennis Brutus)

At three in the afternoon
Two men sit in a room
Facing each other
Over a desk
Overhead a ceiling fan
Whirrs in grey monotone

The man behind the desk
Opens a khaki file
His regulation face creases
Into a visor smile
As he begins his questions

The sole witness —
The fan — raises no objections

Five hours later
The fan squeaks to a halt

And a man can be seen
Stumbling into the night
As the clock strikes eight

Spiral of fan and questions
In the room have ended
Now the questions like the fan
Spin deliriously in a broken
                        man's head.

Abbreviating problems

*Indonesia's Logistics Board (Bulog) has decided to dispense with the term "starvation" (*Kelaparan*) as a stage in critical food conditions. It has opted for "more refined" expressions instead. The first stage is "the possibility of being short of food" or* kemungkinan kurang makan *with its abbreviation, KKM. This is to be used for people who only eat once a day. For those uncertain of getting one meal a day, the official term is to be "short of food" or* kurang makan *(KM).* Hongeroedeem *(HO) will be used for those with swollen bellies, no longer capable of moving.*

Tapol

Words are bombs
and some like *hunger*
kwashiorkor, starvation
often explode in
most unlikely places —
start up a revolution.

Shrewd generals know this:
knowing also that words
will not be contained
behind barbed wire fences
they resort to linguistic devices

Economics of the day
say it is cheaper
to abbreviate than
alleviate the problem.

But *starvation* by
any other name
is still *starvation*:
cannot be wished away
by simple abbreviation.

And abbreviations too —
no matter KKM, KM, HO
or what have you —
can sometimes like TNT
prove positively incendiary!

Nothing's relative

True, there are no earthquakes
as in Nicaragua; nor pestilence...
and plague and locusts have spared us.

And though the sun hammers
without pity in the dry season
and it rains curtains in the wet
flood and drought have yet
to look upon us with unkindly eye.

True, there are no hurricanes
typhoons or ravaging famines;
and there's been no civil war
on the scale of a bloody Biafra.

True, this land has escaped
the excesses of a Hitler
Pol Pot, Idi Amin or Bokassa.

And our people are grateful
for all these myriad mercies.

Still, there are other demons;
and the hunger in the eye
of one beggar-child shames
the conscience of every citizen.

North/South

Life is contradiction.
From moment of birth
over each head
a death sentence hangs.

No matter what path
we take — we're dead!
Carrion for maggots
or ashes in a grate.

So why can't we meet
with cold philosophic eye
news that in a bumper
season they torch wheat-

fields in the North
to keep prices up;
while down the wretched
South, a winter forest

of dark limbs, scored
by desert winds and famine,
moves listless across sand.
In our global village,

these tales of hunger
and surfeit dribble
like trails of snail-
slime in a queasy mind.

Voice of the dispossessed

They
who never knew hunger
spend more
on a night's drinking
than the monthly
wage of a rubber tapper

They
would speak for us
Can the blind see
for the dumb?
Can the dumb talk?

They
who always had shelter
live in palaces
are driven to air-
conditioned offices
by a uniformed chauffeur

They
would speak for us
Can the blind see
for the dumb?
Can the dumb talk?

They
privileged by education
who know the sorcery of words
who can tell the nuances
between Law and Justice —
those twins often in opposition

They
would speak for us
Can the blind see
for the dumb?
Can the dumb talk?

Too late we discover
we were suckered
by their posters
for now secure
in their 5-year tenure
snug in velvet chairs
what do they care
for our pleas and prayers?

After the elections
came the evictions
After the evictions
... the demolitions

The blind can't see
for the dumb
the dumb can't talk
For Justice
has lost her tongue
And Poverty
has no voice...

Turncoats

They who promised cliche
dreams:
Liberty, Fraternity, Equality...

They who pledged the usual
deliverance
from manacles of censorship
incarceration without a trial
restrictions on assembly...

They who made obligatory
noises against the corruption
and greed of rabid colonizers...

They who vowed a land
where shoulder to shoulder
men would one day stand
each equal, proud and free...

Now, all too predictably,
in that "promised land"
over smart lounge suits wear
the mantle of past oppressors.

And all our dreams have gone
rancid under the turncoat sun
and hope is a grain of sand
that grates between one's teeth.

By waters of the Tembeling

(for Ong Soo Keat)

I.

By waters of the Tembeling
where sambar deer
and seladang undisturbed roam
where buffalo
tapir and the wild boar play...

By waters of the Tembeling
where drongo
and hornbill criss-cross skies
where bamboo
genuflects to kiss the river...

By waters of the Tembeling
where lives of
man, bird, beast and flower
intertwine with
grace and beauty like lianas...

By waters of the Tembeling
my mind roamed
across our gauche and grace-
less cities —
their emissaries of greed
and destruction;
a flotilla of timber lorries.

And by the waters
        of the Tembeling
                i sat down and wept.

II.

No piranha menace
the waters
of the Tembeling
but sharks
with buzz-saw teeth
are everywhere...

As the mist lifted off
Bukit Teresek
i saw a once virgin
jungle in dishabille:
torn, ravished, bruised
Used by gangs
of loggers, she lay in
tatters, while
lascivious one-eyed heli-
copters circled
overhead and ogled.

From her lacerated
side i watched
a stream of laterite
trickle to bloody
the waters of Tembeling.

As the mist lifted off
Bukit Teresek
i heard the witches'
whine
of chain-saw cutter.

Clack
and cackle of bulldozer
cracked
the song of bulbul
and cricket.
i saw juggernauts in
every corner
set about dismantling
our forest.

A cirrus of diesel
hovered like a vulture
waiting to take over
this land and its people.

No piranha menace
the waters
of the Tembeling
but sharks
with buzz-saw teeth
are everywhere...

Kali and the caves
(for Gurmit Singh)

So much for the old gods
So much for their ancient
caves, reverence of land,
respect for faith, heritage
history, beauty, ecology...
So much for the old gods.

Hail the new God!
Hail mutant of Kali!

Our new God
sits atop a skyscraper
has a terrible visage
speaks in voice of thunder.

Our new God
eats mountains, forests
regurgitates quarries
spits motorways, mortar
supermarkets, factories.
Our new God's
chariot is a bulldozer.

Ministers of this new
God's ministry do not
wear saffron robes
or clerical collars
but bushjackets
and sport briefcases.
They are all power-
ful and always right.

So, the new God's voice
booming fire and dynamite
prevails over the old gods
and four hundred and forty
million years of history
of stalactite and stalagmite
are blasted into obscurity...

Hail the new God!
Hail mutant of Kali!

Ecological suicide

The village
        deserted.
                The river
choked and polluted.
                And a red
haze hovers
        over devastated
hills.
    But this is not
               the work
of barbarians
        from the north
nor B.29 bombers
            nor foreign
              devils.
In this instance
        we are the authors
of our own death;
        our own nemesis.

Requiem for a rainforest

i wrestle with a rhinoceros
but no words will come

i hear tall trees crashing
wild birds screeching
the buffalo stampeding
but no words will come

i hear sawmills buzzing
cash registers clicking
entrepreneurs chuckling
but no words will come

i hear of press conferences
of petitions, of signatures
of campaigns and lobbying
but no words will come

i hear the rain pounding
into desolate spaces
the widowed wind howling
but no words will come

the rhino is boxed and crated
merbok and meranti are gone
above, no monkeys swing
from no overhead branches
below, a pangolin stumbles
around amputated trunks
an orphaned butterfly
surveys the wounded jungle

yes, no words can fill
this gash of malevolence
but a terrible anger squats
hugging its knees in silence.

All that's gone and been

One rock in particular
i remember well
hippopotamus-humped
jutting belligerently
into the retreating sea.

Ah, if rocks could speak
what stories they would tell
of all that's gone and been
of days of gold and green:
that lush fringe of palm
and cashew and coconut trees
that sash of unsullied sand.

Time was when this beach
was so rich in cockles
a flick of a child's foot
would yield a handful.

Time is when you scuff
the murky sand to find
broken bottles, rusty Coca-
Cola cans, prophylactics
embedded ankle-deep in slime.

And time is when concrete
and steel conceits of man
besiege my placid hippo-
potamus-humped friend.
(Marks though they be of
progress and prosperity
yet who can match her
rugged uncosmetic beauty?)

And yes, at night
unable to hold her silence
you should hear how
with the tongues of waves
she roars her protest
at the insane passing
of all that's gone and been
of those days of gold and green

Time past

"We need to reclaim from the state much greater
control over our own destiny. We have become sub-
jects not citizens of our country."

We move forward in time
backward in sensitivity.

These are days of condo-
miniums and calculators

Days when brokers play
poker with our destiny

In our rush to "progress"
we bulldoze history...

We consign our best
to the rubbish heap

of nostalgia and memory.

* * *

As clouds of dust
billow from stones

that once linked
present to past...

you ache for days
when life like traffic

had a human face;
those days of rick-
shaws and tramcars
of cantered pace

when traffic cops
wore rattan wings.

Time too of reflection
and thoughtful planning

of sculptured courtyards
and palm-lined boulevards

when we were Citizens
not pawns/playthings

when bankers and developers
were not our puppetmasters

when our City Fathers
remembered their children.

Pearl of the Orient

(In memory of Maria Victoria Herrera, runner-up in a "Miss Pearl of the Orient" beauty contest who hung herself in a bedroom closet after being raped by the organizers; and also in memory of an island i once knew.)

Pearl of the Orient
lovely lady, lovely island...

by powerful strings
manipulated
jerked this way
and that;
traumatized
by puppetmasters
who promise dreams
and deliver dust.

Pearl of the Orient
lovely lady, lovely island...

pawed, clawed
ripped, raped
aborted;
your beauty
trampled by swine
who know nothing
of love
only lust and avarice.

Pearl of the Orient
lovely lady, lovely island...

on all sides
massacred
how they used you
abused you
left you bleeding;
that once
virgin body
now dangles like
a broken marionette
in the closet of memory.

Pearl of the orient
lovely lady, lovely island...

On not being able to write a poem celebrating the erection of another multi-storeyed complex

A blade of grass
A grain of rice
A wild flower...

Things that pulse
With life
Often move the piper

But concrete, steel
And glass
What can they inspire?

Giant skyscrapers
Stand testimony
To hearts of mortar!

Pages

Under umbrella
of sea-almond tree
leaves turned fla-
vescent by flame-
toothed sun, sea
wind turns pages
of recent past
resurrects history.

Time of crystal
stream and virgin
sand, unbroken
rock, bamboo
and wild cashew
conclave of merbok
and riot of shrubbery.

All gone now
all gone...

Now only reek
of dead water
clogging
conduits of memory

A prescription for development

Our National General Assembly
was in deep mortification.
An insensitive journalist
(from some northern region)
had branded our country
a model of Underdevelopment.

How to gain recognition
as a developed nation
pondered our President.
The answer? — Commission
a group of technocrats
to study, possibly remedy
this intolerable situation.

Months and seminars later they
outlined their prescription:

What you have here, sir
are too many green hills —
a surfeit of lush vegetation.
Trees are fine but unproductive
and hills are an impediment.

There are too many canefields
and too many plantations.
We do not know what development
is, but an agricultural economy
is the badge of underdevelopment.

Your beaches are beautiful, sir
but lack utilization;
there are no tourists, hotels
or any high-rise apartments.

Your streets are traffic-free
and your towns too quiet;
your people seem stress-free
and a trifle too contented.

They eat fruits and vegetable
and drink natural water
which we're shocked to discover
is indecently clean and pure.

So what we recommend, sir —
for your race to development —
is first massive deforestation
followed by massive importation.

You need juggernauts, bull-
dozers and belching factories
condos and fast-food chains
and hordes of snooping tourists.

You must import mineral water
and a medium-sized nuclear reactor;
and a score of foreign psychiatrists
to service your expat industrialists.

We beg your pardon, but pollution
is the hallmark of development.
To qualify as an advanced country
you have to boast a proper degree
of noise/smog/dumps and derangement

With no hesitation, our President
embraced their recommendation.
In ear-muffs he now sits
in a haze-shrouded apartment.

High above, but not quite beyond
the city's teeming shout and bustle;
with a glass of Perrier water
he pops tranquillizers by the bottle.

He has a direct open line
to his Swiss psychiatrist;
keeps an emergency canister
of oxygen taped to his wrist.

But grinning from ear to ear
as he chomps on his hamburger
Mr President is now all glee.
For that damned foreign journalist
has just declared our country,
"The Developing Nation of the Year".

Kuala Juru — death of a village

Here
intimations of death
hang
heavy in the air
Everywhere
there is the stench
of decay and despair

The river
strangled by
exigencies of industrialization
is dying...
and nobody cares

The fish
in the river
poisoned by progress's vomit
are dying...
and nobody cares

The birds
that feed on the fish
in the river
poisoned by
progress's excrement
are dying...
and nobody cares

And so
a once-proud village
sustained
for centuries
by the richness
of this river
dies...
and nobody cares

To that mammon
DEVELOPMENT
our high-priests
sacrifice
our customs
our culture
our traditions
and environment
and nobody cares

We blind mice
We blind mice
see what we've done
see what we've done
we all ran after
Progress's wife
she cut off our heads
with Development's knife
have you ever seen
such fools in your life
as we blind mice?

Drink this scene

Drink this scene
while you can...
these green-carpeted hills
undulating python-like
towards the horizon
the reverential coconut trees
unruly heads bowed
in prayerful homage
to the arrogant sea
that gash of blue-bright water
this ribbon of unsullied sand
where crabs still linger
tango to thrum of wavebeat...

Drink all this while you can
Before the irresistible hand
Of "progress" leaves her grubby
Pawmarks all over our dear land

Our children

*I don't like people to give food as presents because they
disappear. You cannot play with food.*
                        *(10-year-old when asked
                        what he wants for Christmas)*

*17 million children die each year as a direct result of
malnutrition.*
                                        UNICEF report

We have 2 children: a stone
girl and a space-age boy...

Our electric boy is quick, bright
sharp as lightning and eloquent.

His appetite for constant amusement
and titillation is insatiable.

Each X'mas his requests are legion:
a laser gun, digital watch, remote

control car and kit for space invasion.
But don't give me food as presents,

he admonishes, they soon disappear;
You can't play with food, he reckons.

No, you cannot play with food
our little stone girl will agree

as gargoyle-like she crouches
in unsmiling wide-eyed silence.

Empty bowl in tiny brittle hands
whittled to bone by malnutrition.

She has no dreams of toys and
asks for nothing; but the hunger

(not metaphorical) in her eye
says all there is to say: the only
gift i and my seventeen million other
brothers and sisters need each year

is urgent loving care and a full belly
or we may, all of us, soon disappear...

Asian airport art

Picture a typical rustic scene: 4
cows, 2 bulls, 1 heifer — all well-
fed — grazing on hills of lush green.
1 smiling mother in a floral sarong
(frangipani tucked behind her ear)
suckling 1 contented moon-faced baby.
3 village damsels — buxom, of course —
frolicking by a stream of liquid crystal.
4 atap huts — modest, but inviting —
nestling in a grove of over-laden
coconut, cashew, banana and guava trees.

The whole pictorial cliche neatly boxed
in a frame — twenty-eight by twenty-four.

The village of this artist's inspiration
told a different story: i could count
the ribs of the emaciated cattle as they
wandered listless on the slopes of rust-
coloured, dust-covered, sun-sucked hills.
The mother — lungs racked by t.b. — spat
intermittently into a sewer of stagnant
putrid water — our artist's crystal stream.
There was no frangipani in her hair
and the child in her arms had beri-beri.
And I found no dancing damsels anywhere
nor birdsong nor children's laughter in
this knot of broken shacks and barren trees.

Our celebrated artist had cancelled the pain
                         from his paintings
And now his canvases were a legacy of empty tings.

Beyond nationalism
(for K.J. Ratnam)

From distances shorter
than the moon
continents are a blur
you cannot tell
one country from another.

Seen from the stars
how absurd we seem
with our border wars
— petty squabbles
over neighbours' fences.

We are so small
no more than neutrons
on a speck of dust
floating in the galaxy;
still we're asked
to thump our chest
trumpet our nationality.

Splitting of the shirts

In the Tailor's showcase
all shirts hung equal:
royal shantung rubbed shoulders
with common cotton and polyester
long-sleeves jostled short-sleeves
white mingled freely with coloureds.

At the laundry, it was
a different story: LONG —
SHORT — WHITE — NON-WHITE —
LINEN — COTTON — NYLON — SILK
indelibly marked each was
thrown into a separate basket.

In our Dhobi's cupboard
soon there was chaos.
Given their new status
shantung would have nothing
to do with cotton or linen
long wrestled short and white
was up in arms against coloured.

Dhobi sought Tailor's intervention;
wanted to know the secret of
harmony at latter's establishment.
There is no secret, said Tailor,
in my shop there's no distinction
between any of my many creations.
One breeds hate, it is not innate;
those who sow seeds of separatism
reap the whirlwind of polarization.

A squatter's lament
(for Arumugam)

What will i have left
    of this land
hacked from mangrove
salvaged from wilderness?

    This earth
invested with years/tears
irrigated by blood/sweat

What will i have left
    of this land
that blossomed in my hands
into a carnival of papayas?

    This earth
which nurtured my children
succoured cow, goat, chicken...

What will i have left
    of this land
on that day they tear
her from my calloused hands?

    This earth
i've loved more than
i've loved any woman.

Will i be left anything
    other than
that cupful of clay
that clings to my toes?
that crescent of grit
that moons my fingertips?

Instructions to "true" poets

Seventeen million dead children: not just an unpleasant thought, but a horrible reality. In the past year while most of the world fretted over rising inflation etc., that's how many children died on this planet:
40,000 a day, 1,666 an hour, 27 a minute, one every 2.2 seconds.

Asiaweek

Damn, damn all cliches
race, blood, famine
and such fleeting things.
Record for posterity
the eternal verities
Love, sex, loneliness
the loss of innocence
precious little things.

Write about how she turned
and stomped out leaving
the garden gate unhinged;
write about the terrible pain
of grandpa's ingrown toenail
of the angst and anguish
of some long distance novelist...

Write about death
(if you must)
but keep it personal
and in proportion
an aunt or two
or a distant uncle
never of an entire people
of some bloody foreign nation.

Stick to precious little things
i mean love, sex, loneliness
the loss of innocence...
not bleeding matchstick babies!

And if someone says 17 million
die each year of malnutrition
(one every two seconds)
that's someone else's problem.

You must concentrate on precious
things like love and loneliness;
you must steer clear of obnoxious
cliches like blood and dying children.

Care...

The image: familiar
babies whittled
to hybrid insects —
beetle-bellies glued
to spider limbs —
by that demon hunger.

The silence: terrifying
as the photograph
in the Sunday newspaper
no songs, no games
no blind-man's-buff
not an echo of laughter

So easy to turn the page
shelve the horror
but if we do not care
for a neighbour's child
today, who will care
for our children tomorrow?

Oil perspectives

When the oil prices
went up...

the two-car lawyer in
his smart carpeted
air-conditioned office
ranted against OPEC
now that the "crisis"
had trimmed his wife's
afternoon shopping sprees

the one-sampan fisherman
in his atap shack
quietly snuffed out his
second kerosene lamp
gave thanks to Allah
he still had some light

Sensitive

To have a "sensitive soul"
(as some fortunate poets do)
is a commendable thing,
we're told, enables them to
spin fine sentences, win claps
and prestigious literary kudos

To raise a "sensitive issue"
is however, not so admirable;
it's the kind of stuff sub-
versives do, claps them in
handcuffs, wins them long
sentences behind steel doors!

Apathy

Living in the flabby
midriff of this country
senses are lulled
into a kind of stupor

Sipping rare brandy
from a $500 decanter
impossible to imagine
a gangrene called hunger

And poverty is another planet...

When suddenly a small girl
wilts from debility under
the sun and strangles you
with her frail whimper

Past the plush, private clinics
a near hysterical mother
rushes her twitching child
to the hospital in a trisha

And a question hovers...

Conscience pickled in vodka
when Armageddon comes
how will you explain your
indifference to your Maker?

Tide

Turned by wind
foam-lipped
waves flap
against sand
like pages of a
well-thumbed book

And from under
umbrella of sea-
almond tree
my mind flaps
back through
leaves of history.

Rumours whisper
this precise spot
was the location
our fathers mapped
our Constitution
drew up plans
to overthrow
the colonial master.

Liberty,
Fraternity
Equality...
how easy to
champion ideals
when the dog
of imperialism
was snapping
at our heels.

History and the tide
have turned. Cast
further up the beach,
feet in flotsam, i ask:
Where are those dreams?

Seaspray and spume
foam and froth
crashing against rocks.

The pawnbrokers

Where are those dreams
haframed with such eloquence
across the water?

Where are those orisons
of justice forged
in righteous anger?

Where are those hearts
pulsating as one
in selfless fire?

Gone, gone in the mud
each and everyone
lost in the mire

Studying the Race-form
sipping wine
knocking back the beer

Made fat by our silences
do we still dare point
an accusing finger?

We hypocritical fools who
have hawked our souls
for silver

Who have pledged our pearls
for the stercoral stench
of the sewer

Holiday snapshot

It was certainly one
for the holiday album;
a postcard advertisement
for coca-cola and rum.
A palm-fringed bay
with yachts of prosperity
tacking in the breeze;
the dollar buoyant;

while everywhere
that smell of affluence
— sweat and sun-tan lotion —
rising off bodies

pinking in the sun
like lobsters on a spit.
A postcard advertisement
for coca-cola and rum.

No camera recorded
the sharks of greed;
the weed of deception
a deceit beneath surfaces.

There was no indication
of the martial fist
that composed this picture
to lure the tourist.

It was certainly one
for the holiday album
a postcard advertisement
for coca-cola and rum.

A different death

I have a wife
a son, daughter
sisters, brother
and an extended family

But if these be
my only loves
then cut me up
and feed me
to the dogs
I am dead

In my garden
grow papayas
and watermelons
and bougainvillaeas
bloom in mad profusion

But if these prove
my sole distraction
then cut me up
and feed me
to the dogs
I am dead

I have a thirst
for poetry
rhythm, music...
a hunger for
casuarinas
and the wild sea

but if these be
all my wants
then cut me up
and feed me
to the dogs
I am dead

I have a job
that pays well
food in my belly
a bank account
a roof over my head

If I demand less
for any other man
then cut me up
and feed me
to the dogs
I am dead dead dead

In memoriam
(for Sen. Jose "Pepe" Diokno)

Framing a perfect metaphor
a protracted twilight
of blood and gold
bannered the horizon
on the day of your departure.

Serving as if to remind us
of the richness and wretchedness
of our lands, Pepe, to which
you bore such eloquent witness.

In a continent of mincing minions
and dancing marionettes
who for a fee or a favour
will serve any puppetmaster
you were the most independent of lions.

And now that you are gone
our loss is streaked with fear.
The struggle is far from over;
with so much work, yet to be done
who will be our touchstone, our lodestar?

Note: One of Asia's most indefatigable champions of human
rights, Senator Jose Diokno, founder of FLAG (Free Legal Assist-
ance Group), was also a pioneer of free legal aid in the region. An
intractable opponent of martial law and a brilliant lawyer, he was
imprisoned by Ferdinand Marcos for defending Benigno Aquino
and others opposed to that dictatorship. He was Chairman of the
Presidential Commission on Human Rights at the time of his death
on 27 February 1987.

Home and abroad

The climate is Fear.
Threats, real and imaginary
are conjured to mascara
the nation's future.

Then, legislation tightens
its noose on the citizen.
It's a State of Emergency.
We must all be vigilant.

A sudden change of weather
for the foreign investor.
The charcoal clouds roll...
everything's under control.

Our investment climate
could not be brighter.
It's definitely an area
of Freedom, Peace and Security.

Dancing on the ceiling

i will dance on fire
but i will not dance
where the lawyer
abdicates responsibility
to play footsie
with the politician
for pewterplates and position.

i will dance underwater
but i will not dance
on slime and excreta-
slicked beaches
colonized by cohorts
of rats and cockroaches.

i will dance in limbo
but i will not dance
where racism slow
foxtrots, cheek to
jowl with expediency
to the strains of some
cockeyed National Policy.

i will dance on phosphorous
but i will not dance
where the androgynous
architect visits his
phallic fantasy
to camouflage
an ambivalent sexuality.

i will dance on the ceiling
but i will not dance
in courtyards ringing
the shrill screams
of the tortured
in stadiums dripping
the thick blood of patriots...

i will dance on the wind
but i will not dance
at a radiation binge
where hopes turn
rancid in the womb
and all our dreams
and tomorrows are entombed.

Glossary

Ang-pow	A red packet containing money given during Chinese New Year.
Batu caves	These are among the world's most historic limestone caves, some 440 million years old, now threatened by limestone quarrying. The caves are not only treasure houses of historical and ecological data but also house the temple of Lord Murugan, an Indian deity.
Bearing scraper	A slim three-edged tool used by motor mechanics for cleaning engine bearings but now commonly used as a lethal weapon in gang warfare.
Boria	A local song/dance presentation in fancy dress. The songs usually are humorous and topical.
Bukit Terasek	A small hill.
Drongo	An exotic bird.
Gurmit Singh	Malaysia's leading environmentalist who played a major role in the fight to save the Batu caves.
Kali	The goddess of destruction in the Hindu pantheon.
Kebaya	A fine local blouse worn with a sarong.
Merbok	A type of Malaysian ground-dove noted for its singing.
Ong Soo Keat	Malaysia's foremost wildlife artist.
Seladang	Wild buffalo.
Tembeling	A river that runs through the heart of the Malaysian National Park which is threatened by logging and a proposed hydro-electric scheme.
Trisha	A local three-wheeled pedalled conveyance.

Some other Risk books *

John S. Pobee — **WHO ARE THE POOR?**
The Beatitudes as a call to community

C.F. Beyers Naudé and Dorothee Sölle — **HOPE FOR FAITH**
A conversation

Masao Takenaka — **GOD IS RICE**
Asian culture and Christian faith

André Jacques — **THE STRANGER WITHIN YOUR GATES**
Uprooted people in the world today

S. Wesley Ariarajah — **THE BIBLE AND PEOPLE OF OTHER FAITHS**

John V. Taylor — **WEEP NOT FOR ME**
Meditations on the cross and the resurrection

Zephania Kameeta — **WHY, O LORD?**
Psalms and sermons from Namibia

Emilio Castro — **SENT FREE**
Mission and unity in the perspective of the kingdom

Joan Puls, O.S.F. — **EVERY BUSH IS BURNING**
A spirituality for our times

Michael Kinnamon — **WHY IT MATTERS**
Personal reflections on the "Baptism, Eucharist and Ministry" text

Allan Boesak — **WALKING ON THORNS**
The call to Christian obedience

---

* Available from WCC Publications

W.J. Milligan — **THE NEW NOMADS**
Challenges facing Christians in western Europe

John Bluck — **BEYOND TECHNOLOGY**
Contexts for Christian communication

Cecil Rajendra — **SONGS FOR THE UNSUNG**
Poems on unpoetic issues like war, want and refugees

Lesslie Newbigin — **THE OTHER SIDE OF 1984**
Questions to the churches

Claudius — **ONCE UPON A TIME...**
Political fables

Rodney M. Booth — **THE WINDS OF GOD**
The Canadian churches face the 1980s

Betty Thompson — **A CHANCE TO CHANGE**
Women and men in the church

John J. Vincent — **STARTING ALL OVER AGAIN**
Hints of Jesus in the city

C.S. Song — **THE TEARS OF LADY MENG**
A parable of people's political theology

Marianne Katoppo — **COMPASSIONATE AND FREE**
An Asian woman's theology

Albert H. van den Heuvel — **SHALOM AND COMBAT**
A personal struggle against racism

Rex Davis — **LOCUSTS AND WILD HONEY**
The charismatic renewal and the ecumenical movement